His Word

To Joe and Arlene —
In His love — Words
can't express what I
owe you and how much
I admire you. Pray
for me

Fr David Knight

His Word

Letting It Take Root
—and Bear Fruit—
in Our Lives

David Knight

Nihil Obstat: Rev. Hilarion Kistner, O.F.M.
                  Rev. John J. Jennings

Imprimi Potest: Rev. Jeremy Harrington, O.F.M.
                    Provincial

Imprimatur: †James H. Garland, V.G.
                Archdiocese of Cincinnati
                December 3, 1985

Book design and cover by Julie Lonneman.

SBN 0-89716-048-9

© 1986, David Knight
All rights reserved.
Published by St. Anthony Messenger Press.
Printed in the U.S.A.

Contents

To Joe and Arlene Kelly,
whose response to *His Way*
is one of my greatest consolations—
and in whose house I wrote this book.

Introduction

A few years ago I wrote a book called *His Way*. It turned out to be my most popular book and, quite frankly, the response it evoked overwhelmed me.

People began to use it in discussion groups, so I wrote a guidebook called *To Follow His Way*. But when they finished their discussions, frequently someone would call me and say, "We've finished *His Way* and *To Follow His Way*, but our group wants to continue meeting. We would like to go into Scripture now. What would you recommend?"

My response to that was joy. In my mind, the logical follow-up to *His Way*—the logical first step, anyway—is to start reading and praying over Scripture. I believe that the choice to do this is the first serious step toward leading a conscious, growth-producing spiritual life.

The Scriptures are the Word of life. Jesus compares his words to seeds: Where they are nurtured and grow, they produce fruit. Many people, however, are disappointed when they begin to read the Word of God. They start, they expect great things to take place, and nothing happens. So they stop.

They may not consciously put the blame on God's Word. They may take the blame themselves, saying something like, "Well, I just don't get anything out of it. Maybe I don't know how to pray over Scripture. Maybe it's not the thing for me."

But I can't help believing that somewhere down deep they are also disappointed in Scripture itself. "If this is the Word of God, why isn't it doing for me what it has done for others? What is there about Scripture reading that is supposed to be so special?"

Such a question isn't limited to Scripture. It can be asked—in fact, it is constantly being asked—about the life of grace itself: "If religion is so great, how come it hasn't helped me?" "Twelve years in a Catholic school, and my kids all left the Church. What's wrong?" "Christianity has been around for 2,000 years, and look at the mess the world is in!"

Underlying this bewilderment is a doubt: If Jesus really was the Savior, then obviously his followers have not been able to carry on his work, to live out his Word. But if his followers have not been able to carry on his work, was he really the Savior in the first place?

This book attempts to speak to this doubt. For Jesus *is* the Savior. His Word *can* make great things happen. It *can* transform our lives. It *can* turn the world around. The problem is not that Jesus' Word is impotent but that his Word has rarely been heard. And the reason for this is that certain stumbling blocks in our lives hinder our receptivity to his Word.

This is a book, then, not on how to *read* the Scriptures, but on how to *respond* to the Scriptures, and therefore how to respond to the life of grace itself. It tries to show how we can let the Word of God take root in our hearts, live and flourish there, and bear fruit in Christian action.

The content of this book is taken from our Lord's own teaching about grace as a growing thing. In the Parable of the Sower and the Seed (Matthew 13:4-8) Jesus gives three reasons why his Word fails to bear fruit in people's hearts. And he points toward the one thing (as I interpret this passage, at least) which, more than anything else, helps us to become and to remain "good ground" for the growth of his Word. Exploring these three reasons for failure and this one formula for success will be the content of this book.

This book can serve either individuals, reading and reflecting alone, or groups who meet to discuss it. The Questions for Reflection and Discussion at the end of each chapter are designed to help individuals or groups consolidate what they have read and then respond to it through choices.

This reflection is important: Words merely read are a waste of time. Words read and understood are pure potential. Words reflected upon until they bring us to a point of choice are words of life. And choices are the forward motion of life. I hope that the words in this book lead to choices that help make our hearts fertile ground for cultivating His Word.

The Parable of the Sower and the Seed
Making the Kingdom Come

The Reign of God is a mystery. We may feel that the greatest mystery about it is why it hasn't worked. Why haven't the fantastic promises made in the Old Testament about the Messiah been fulfilled?

> In days to come,
> The mountain of the LORD's house
>   shall be established as the highest mountain
>   and raised above the hills.
> All nations shall stream toward it;
>   many peoples shall come and say:
> "Come, let us climb the LORD's mountain,
>   to the house of the God of Jacob,
> That he may instruct us in his ways,
>   and we may walk in his paths."
> For from Zion shall go forth instruction,
>   and the word of the LORD from Jerusalem.
> He shall judge between the nations,
>   and impose terms on many peoples.
> They shall beat their swords into plowshares
>   and their spears into pruning hooks;
> One nation shall not raise the sword against another,
>   nor shall they train for war again. (Isaiah 2:2-4)

In the light of today's reality, this text seems almost sarcastic. What nation is *not* raising the sword against another? What nation is *not* training for war? And where is this great stream of people clamoring to be instructed in the ways of the Lord?

This problem is not unique to our times. The disciples of Jesus continually raised the same question, not only in the early Church, but even during the lifetime of Jesus himself! Despite the enthusiastic responses that sometimes followed a sermon or a miracle (see Matthew 4:23-25; 7:28-29; Acts 2:41; 13:48-49), the general response to the Good News was not that overwhelming (see, for example, Matthew 11:16-20; 13:54-58; Acts 13:50; 17:32-34; 22:22-23).

So it isn't surprising that the disciples would sometimes wonder just how effective a Savior Jesus was. In fact, Scripture scholars say that when Jesus told the Parable of the Sower and the Seed (see Matthew 13:1-23), it was probably in answer to the question from one of his disciples, "If you are the Messiah, why isn't anyone listening to you? Why do you have so few followers?"

For Jesus' contemporaries and for us today the Parable of the Sower presents a revolutionary concept: The Kingdom will not be established by God alone; it will be the joint product of God's divine giving and our human receptivity, of God's power and our free surrender, of God's all-powerful Word and our willing response. The grace to make this response will be given, but it will not be imposed.

In other words, Jesus was and is a Savior whose power to save is limited in practice by our willingness to accept salvation. His power to transform our lives is limited by our willingness to cooperate in being transformed. The Kingdom of God is established by Jesus working through his Body on earth, which is us. God chooses to reign on this earth in respectful dependence on us.

The Parable

Let's take a closer look at this Parable of the Sower and the Seed:

"One day a farmer went out sowing. Part of what he sowed landed on a footpath, where birds came and ate it up. Part of it fell on rocky ground, where it had little soil. It sprouted at once since the soil had no depth, but when the sun rose and scorched it, it began to wither for lack of roots. Again, part of the seed fell among thorns, which grew up and choked it. Part of it, finally, landed on good soil and yielded grain a hundred- or sixty- or thirtyfold." (Matthew 13:4-8)

God sows his Reign through his words, like seeds. There is nothing defective about the seed—it is powerful, lifegiving, divine. But the seed will not take root and bear fruit unless it is received into good ground. The Kingdom is the fruit of divine invitation and free, human response.

So God does not impose his Reign with power, unilaterally, subjecting the whole human race to himself and establishing his order, his peace on earth. The Reign of God, as Jesus teaches it, is not domination; it is a covenant, a joint creation. It is made up of God's free invitation and the free acceptance of every human person. No one comes under the Reign of God except through a willing, personal surrender.

Although the Reign of God which Jesus preached will not be imposed by force, it will be established with power, but the power is totally different from anything the world understands by that word. Rather than the power of domination, it is the winning, enabling, liberating power of grace and of love.

This is the mystery of God's Reign. It is a mystery of the human and the divine made one, of God's acting humanly through us and our acting divinely "in Christ."

Faith in the Incarnation

This mystery calls for fantastic faith—not just in God's power to do all things, but in his power to enable *us* to do them. We must believe in Jesus Christ: that he was truly God and truly man, that in him the infinite power of God and the limited abilities of a human being existed together without either one effacing the other. Our faith in the Incarnation tells us that Jesus really was limited in what he could do—what he could learn, understand, accomplish and endure—by his divinity acting in and through his human nature. Yet this human being—who in every way felt and thought, understood and chose, acted and experienced life just as we do (see Hebrews 2:16-18; 4:15-16)—was at the same time the very person of the infinite God made flesh.

It is easier to believe in God than to believe in divinized humanity—whether it be the humanity of Jesus who was divine by his very being, or our own humanity (that of the Church on earth) made divine by grace. It is easier to believe in a Kingdom to be established by God's almighty power acting alone, than in a Kingdom to be established by God's power working through the weakness of ordinary human beings made extraordinary through grace (see 1 Corinthians 1:18—2:16).

The mystery of God's Reign, as Jesus actually inaugurated it, is a mystery of human beings doing what only God can do, because these human beings have become sharers, through grace, in the life and power of God.

There would be no challenge to our faith if this divine power that is given us simply overrode our human nature. If God simply enlightened our minds by grace, without requiring any human education, reflection or understanding, then we would know by the power of God, and all Christians would speak with the manifest wisdom of divine enlightenment. There would be no human groping for clarification, for the right words to express divine revelation, for the right theological formula or the right decision in the complicated moral situations of this world. All Christians would be oracles: God would speak through them as through inanimate statues, without their needing to use their human equipment at all.

The children of light would be perfectly distinguishable from the children of darkness, because they would always be right: effortlessly, unerringly,

8

exhaustively. The divine gift of grace would be so obvious no one could fail to recognize it. God's power would shine out, not as working through the limitations of human nature, but as simply sweeping aside those limitations. But this is not Incarnation.

Grace Working Through the Human

The true mystery of God-in-human-flesh (whether in Jesus or in us) is the mystery of God doing the divine through the limited and laborious operation of the human powers he endowed us with by nature. God dwelling in us by grace assists our minds and wills divinely in their human acts of thinking and choosing, so that little by little our understanding is clarified, our attitudes are reshaped, our priorities are rearranged, and our actions become more like God's.

This happens so slowly that sometimes the divine working of grace is hardly recognizable. In individuals it may take place over a period of years; in the Church, in the People of God as a whole, it may take place over a period of centuries. A true transformation is going on. It is the work of God, but of God working at a human pace. That is why we often fail to see it happening.

Grace working through nature transforms us gradually—the way all human change takes place. The words of Jesus spoken in the first century may raise a problem in the second century that is answered fundamentally in the third century, then clarified and expanded upon in every century thereafter.

The same is true of the Church's action: A practice that is universal in the world in the first century (owning slaves, for example) may be recognized by Christians as problematic only several centuries later (as was slavery in the 18th century). When the practice is finally condemned (probably, as in the case of slavery, with the help of a number of human factors not all exclusively Christian— such as economic changes, political movements, literary creations, philosophical debates and other developments of cultural evolution), the influence of Christianity as such may hardly be noticed. In fact, the Christian conscience may seem to have been formed more by the insights of nonbelievers than vice versa.

But often, even when the practice is supposedly abolished, that is not the end of it. It may take centuries more even for the majority of Christians to accept the new way of thinking. The Church is the human-divine Body of Christ on earth, and it takes time for the members to adjust to new directions from the head.

We have a classic example of this in the resistance of some early Christians to the Church's decision not to impose the rules of Judaism on Gentile converts. The struggle to free the Church from the restrictions of the Mosaic Law is reflected in all the Gospels and was a preoccupation of St. Paul during his entire preaching career (see, for example, Matthew 12:1-15; 23:1-39; Acts 15:1-32; Romans 2:17 ff.; Galatians 2:1—3:1). Even in a Church which is the divine Body of Christ on earth, the momentum of human inertia is not instantly reversed.

Finally, the Church's first responses to a problem may themselves by flawed by sin (as the abolition of slavery was flawed by segregation, for example). Only gradually is the human heart purified of false attitudes, wrong values and unjust priorities in this world. But this is the way grace works: almost imperceptibly, and at a human pace.

That is why the Kingdom is never fully established in any age or place or culture, whether in the speculative area of truth or in the practical area of justice. The Reign of God over every area of human life and activity is always *being* established; the Kingdom is always "at hand." It will not actually "be here" in its completeness until Christ comes again.

A Call to Action

In the meantime, Christ will reign on earth only in the measure that we give ourselves humanly to being his Body. This means dedicating ourselves in active, human ways to putting on the mind of Christ (see Philippians 2:5;

1 Corinthians 2:14-16; Romans 13:14; Ephesians 4:1-24)—to reflecting on his words, giving up old attitudes and values, taking on the goals and priorities of Jesus in everything we do, modeling our life-styles after the example he set, working to reform and restructure society according to the principles of his teaching.

To do this is to embody faith in action. Our faith becomes fully real only when it is expressed in decisions and choices. Salvation is founded on the Word made flesh. To extend salvation—and the Reign of Jesus Christ—to the whole world we must make Christ's words flesh in every area of human life and activity by embodying them in our human actions.

So why hasn't Christ's salvation worked? Why is the world not changed? Why are we ourselves so far from experiencing, from realizing in our own lives the promises of his Kingdom? The answer is not that the words of Jesus do not work. The answer is that we have not worked to put them to work—in our own hearts and in our world.

The words of God in Scripture are the seed of life; we have our Lord's own word for that. But, like every seed, they need to be nurtured in order to grow. And they need to reach maturity before they bear fruit. Where the seed does not grow to fruitful maturity, it is not because something is lacking in the seed; it is rather that something is lacking in the ground which receives it.

This doesn't mean the ground is bad. It just means it needs to be prepared, tended, cultivated. And that is not as big a job as it may sound. With a minimum of knowledge about spiritual gardening, we can assure that the Word of God will bear fruit in our lives. The rest of this book is designed to show us what we can do to help the seed of Christ's words work and bear fruit in our lives.

Summary

Theme
Our human activity plays a part in establishing the Reign of Christ within ourselves and throughout the world.

Goal
To understand and accept how important it is for us to act in response to the gospel: to take Christ's words seriously in reflection and prayer, to embody them in action in our lives through concrete choices, to commit ourselves to this with new awareness and deeper appreciation.

Key Thoughts

Introduction
  • The Reign of God is a mystery, and we may feel that the greatest mystery about it is why it hasn't worked.

The Parable of the Sower and the Seed
  • The Kingdom is the fruit of divine invitation and free, human response.
  • It is a mystery of the human and the divine made one, of God's acting humanly through us and our acting divinely "in Christ."
  • The Kingdom of God is established by Jesus working through his Body on earth, which is us. God chooses to reign on this earth only in respectful dependence on us.

Faith in the Incarnation
  • It is easier to believe in God than to believe in divinized humanity.
  • It is easier to believe in a Kingdom to be established by God's almighty power acting alone, than in a Kingdom to be established by God's power working through the weakness of ordinary human beings made extraordinary through grace.
  • The mystery of God's Reign, as Jesus actually

inaugurated it, is a mystery of human beings doing what only God can do, because these human beings have become sharers, through grace, in the life and power of God.

Grace Working Through the Human

• The true mystery of God-in-human-flesh is the mystery of God doing the divine through the limited and laborious operation of the human powers he endowed us with by nature.

• The Kingdom is the work of God, but of God working at a human pace. That is why we often fail to see it happening.

• Grace working through nature transforms us gradually—the way all human change takes place.

• That is why the Kingdom is never fully established in any age, place or culture. It is always *being* established; the Kingdom is always "at hand." It will not actually "be here" in its completeness until Christ comes again.

A Call to Action

• Our faith becomes fully real only when it is expressed in decisions and choices.

• The answer to our problem with the Kingdom is not that the words of Jesus do not work. The answer is that we have not worked to put them to work—in our own hearts and in our world.

Questions for Reflection and Discussion

1. Have I ever felt that religion didn't work for me as it should? That I "got nothing" out of reading Scripture or praying?

2. Would I really prefer that God not act in dependence on people's free will? What effect would this have on the value of our lives? Our free choices? Our love?

3. Can I accept in my heart that God acts in me, in others, in his Church at a human pace, waiting on human growth in understanding, generosity, love?

4. How can I cooperate, through the use of my human powers, in God's work of enlightening me, purifying me, sanctifying me?

2.

The Seed That Lands on the Footpath

Breaking From the Cultural 'Beaten Path'

I was once talking to a Ngama tribesman in a vegetable garden in the flat savannah lands of Chad, Africa. In a whimsical mood I picked up a head of lettuce and said, "Ngaradum, is the world round or flat?"

He looked around him at the countryside, as flat as a bedspread in every direction, and said, "It is flat."

"No," I said, "As a matter of fact, it is round—like this head of lettuce."

He just began speaking of sweet potatoes!

We frequently respond to the words of Jesus in the same way. Many of our Lord's sayings just never register because they are totally incompatible with ideas, assumptions and values that are the very foundation of our thinking and our lives. So we never hear them.

It isn't that we understand and reject Jesus' words—consciously. We might feel guilty if we did that. It is just that they do not fit into the system of attitudes and practical working principles that form the structure of our everyday, decision-making lives. They are not compatible with the stance we take toward family life, social life, politics and business policies.

Before we could accept what Jesus is saying, we would have to call into question our whole understanding of the relationship we have with our society. We would have to radically "break" with our culture. Because we are not ready to make such a break, we unconsciously rationalize. Without even facing the particular issue, we assume that Jesus must not really mean what he says.

The Word vs. Cultural Conditioning

Our Lord gives this as the first reason why his words do not produce results: They go contrary to our cultural conditioning.

> "Part of what [the farmer] sowed landed on a footpath, where birds came and ate it up....The seed along the path is the man who hears the message about God's reign without understanding it. The evil one approaches him to steal away what was sown in his mind." (Matthew 13:4, 19)

Whenever the Word of God falls on the hard-beaten path of our cultural conditioning, it just never penetrates. People "look but do not see, they listen but do not hear or understand" (Matthew 13:13). Before the Word is received deeply enough to even address our wills or call us to a decision, it is ejected—like a tape that doesn't fit into our tape recorder. It is not heard and rejected, which would imply understanding and conscious choice; it is simply thrown out before it even has a chance to play its tune.

Psychologists and educators speak of "apperceptive mass." The ancient philosophical principle put it this way: *Quidquid recipitur, secundum modum recipientis recipitur*. That translates: Anything we perceive, we perceive according to our own background and conditioning—and, we might add, according to the personal goals which it threatens or supports. If anyone, even God himself, says something to us which in no way matches our direction in life, or in no way fits into the system of attitudes and values we take for granted, we simply never hear it.

It is not that we hear it, understand it and reject it. We just never hear it. Unconsciously or subconsciously our minds say, "That doesn't make sense; he can't mean that." And the whole idea is just thrown out—"Does not compute."

16

It took Christians more than 1,800 years to see that slavery is incompatible with the gospel. It took almost as long to see that torture of prisoners is a sin. And yet, according to Amnesty International's 1984 report, there are 90 countries today whose governments use torture on political prisoners. Some of the so-called "Catholic" governments of Latin America—which are supported by training and money from the United States—are among the worst offenders.

After 2,000 years of Christianity, why are Christians so unchristian? Why does the Word of God have so little effect? Obviously this question is as much of a problem and a stumbling block to us today as it was to Jesus' own disciples. And the answer the disciples received from Jesus—the Parable of the Sower—is likewise an answer for us.

Jesus tells us in the first part of this answer that when the Word of God falls on the "beaten path" of cultural conditioning, it just never gets a hearing. The "evil one" comes to "steal away what was sown." When people have made their bed with the culture, even the Word of God is frequently unable to penetrate the darkness.

This gives new significance to John's words about the Word of God himself made flesh:

The light shines on in darkness,
a darkness that did not overcome it. (John 1:5)

The "evil one" and the entrenchment of evil in the world can block the reception of God's Word. But the Word of God himself cannot be overcome.

A Pickaxe: The Key to the Kingdom

So the first condition for our entering the Kingdom of God, for our accepting Christ's reign over our hearts, is to declare ourselves emancipated from our culture. We have to take a pickaxe to the beaten path. We have to loosen and turn over the soil so the seed can penetrate.

Like the people of Israel, we have to leave the security of our slavery behind and come out of Egypt. We can allow nothing to determine our lives except the will and the teaching of Jesus Christ:

> "No man can serve two masters. He will either hate one and love the other or be attentive to one and despise the other. You cannot give yourself to God and money." (Matthew 6:24)

Sometime in our lives, and before we can claim to be serious Christians, we have to face this question: By which light will we guide our lives? Will it be the light of this world, which the Gospel defines as darkness (see Matthew 4:16; 6:22-23; John 12:35-46)? Or will it be the light of Christ? This is the first, most basic and most radical choice of our Christian existence.

We cannot march to the music of this world and pick up the new tune of Christ at the same time. We have to choose our drummer. Once we have fallen into Christ's cadence, we can integrate into his music those notes from the world which will harmonize, that is, which can become part of his tune. But first we have to put every tune out of our heads except the one he plays. This is simply a logical consequence and a practical application of the commandment given to our fathers in the desert: "'I, the LORD, am your God....You shall not have other gods besides me'" (Exodus 20:2-3).

This means radical emancipation from culture, a passionate declaration of independence with regard to all the attitudes, values, priorities, goals and assumptions of this world—of our own society and of every other. We are called to the same utter divorce from the world and the same wholehearted devotion to God as the Israelites:

> "Hear, O Israel! The LORD is our God, the LORD alone! Therefore, you shall love the LORD, your God, with all your heart, and with all your soul, and with all your strength." (Deuteronomy 6:4-5).

Pope Paul VI described evangelization in these terms:

> For the Church it is a question not only of preaching the Gospel in ever wider geographic areas or to ever greater numbers of people, but also of affecting and as it were upsetting, through the power of the Gospel, mankind's criteria of judgment, determining values, points of interest, lines of thought, sources of inspiration and models of life, which are in contrast with the Word of God and the plan of salvation.... What matters is to evangelize man's culture and cultures, not in a purely decorative way, by applying a thin veneer, but in a vital way, in depth and right to their very roots. *(Evangelii Nuntiandi, #19-21)*

That calls for a pickaxe.

Jesus was clear and emphatic about this. He overturned the values of his culture—of every human culture—at every level. The opening words of the Sermon on the Mount are an example: "Blessed are the poor in spirit,...the sorrowing,...the lowly...." The Beatitudes are not a set of soothing words to comfort the soul; they are a radical overturning of our whole value system.

There is not one Beatitude which our culture spontaneously believes in or accepts. We do not want to be poor in spirit—or in any other way. We do not want to be sorrowing or lowly. Who, for example, really believes it is a blessing to feel inadequate? But that is what being "poor in spirit" means when brought down to the ground level of practical living.

Christ radically overturns cultural values in all areas of human living:

Financial security and material provisions: "...do not worry about your livelihood, what you are to eat or drink or use for clothing..." (Matthew 6:25; and see Luke 14:13).

Family ties and the closest human relationships: "If anyone comes to me without turning his back on his father and mother, his wife and his children, his brothers and sisters, indeed his very self, he cannot be my follower" (Luke 14:26; and see Matthew 10:37).

Comfort, home and shelter: "The foxes have lairs, the birds in the sky have nests, but the Son of Man has nowhere to lay his head" (Matthew 8:20).

Social obligations, even the most sacred: "Follow me, and let the dead bury their dead" (Matthew 8:22).

Health and the integrity of the body: "If your hand or foot is your undoing, cut it off..." (Matthew 18:8).

Sexual fulfillment and marriage: "Everyone who divorces his wife and marries another commits adultery" (Luke 16:18). "...some there are who have freely renounced sex for the sake of God's reign..." (Matthew 19:12).

Status and prestige: "...unless you change and become like little children, you will not enter the kingdom of God" (Matthew 18:3). "Anyone among you who aspires to greatness must serve the rest..." (Matthew 20:26).

The preservation of life itself: "Whoever would save his life will lose it, but whoever loses his life for my sake will find it" (Matthew 16:25).*

These sayings of Jesus are given here as mind-teasers, as incentives to meditation. They are taken out of context and call for interpretation. Still, they demonstrate that our Lord did not hesitate to call into question the most basic assumptions of his culture—and of ours. We cannot truly "hear" what he is saying unless we are willing to go down to the foundations and rebuild our value system from the ground up.

---

*These examples are adapted from my book *Lift Up Your Eyes to the Mountain,* page 102. In two other books, *Blessed Are They* and *Make Me a Sabbath of Your Heart,* I present the Beatitudes and the Sermon on the Mount in concrete detail as a radical overturning of all human values and a call to live on the level of God himself. (These books are available through His Way, Inc., 1310 Dellwood Ave., Memphis, TN 38127.)

In practice this means that we must set our minds to "wide open"—ready for radical challenge—whenever we read or listen to the Word of God. We have to break open the ground of our hearts—take a pickaxe to it—if we want the seed to penetrate. We have to prepare the soil as a farmer does. And this means taking a stance of radical emancipation—of independence at the roots—with regard to our culture. If we stand on the beaten path, we will never really hear what Jesus says. But if we truly accept Jesus as the Savior of our existence, then we have to be ready to break open any other ground we stand upon.

The 'Decision for Christ'

What can we do, concretely, to declare our emancipation from culture?

We might make a symbolic gesture: We could shave our heads, for example. Or paint our noses blue. Or get a tailor to make us a camel's hair jumpsuit and go on a diet of grasshoppers and wild honey as St. John the Baptist did.

There are any number of symbolic ways to express a break with culture. Most of the really imaginative ones were popularized ages ago by some saint—or have recently become commonplace in California. But just breaking with culture as such is not a particularly Christian act. The simple fact of marching to a different drummer is no guarantee that one is in step with God—or even with reality.

A Christian break with culture is more positive than this. It consists essentially in a radical act of accepting Jesus Christ as Savior.

This might not sound radical at all. Most Christians assume they have already done it. But if one thinks about what this act of acceptance means, it turns out to be a decision which determines the very direction of our lives, and of every other decision we will ever make.

To accept Jesus Christ as Savior means to make an act of faith that *his way* is the right way.

That decision alone is an act of breaking with every

21

culture in the world. It is not the choice of a counterculture, which is just another way to achieve the goals of a good, human life on this earth. It is the choice of a way of life directed from above and directed toward a fulfillment beyond this world. It is a choice of emancipation (though not of rejection or of separation) from human culture as such. It is the choice to live by a light that is not of this world.

In the last analysis, there are only three rational guidance systems anyone can follow in life: one's own opinion, the opinions of other human beings or the revelation of God. We can, therefore, be personalists, cultural conformists or believers. Most of us, I suppose, do not follow consistently any one of these; we blend different ones together and keep switching back and forth.

If for the most part, however, we base our lives on what other people do, or just take for our own the attitudes and values of some other person or group—an expert, the scientific community, our social or cultural milieu, a guru, a philosopher, a sect, a political leader— then we are essentially "followers." We are, as the sociologists say, "other-directed." *Other* people direct our lives.

If, on the other hand, we are in most respects independent thinkers (there is no such thing as a totally independent thinker) and direct our lives by attitudes and values we have thought out for ourselves, weighed interiorly and appropriated as our own, then we are "inner-directed." Our direction comes primarily from within ourselves.

What It Means to Be a Christian
To be a *Christian* does not mean that we cut off either the opinions and wisdom of others or (above all!) the light of our own interior perception. Christians, as a matter of fact, accept bonds of unity and even of unanimity with the whole body of believers. There is a strong sense of identification with the community of the Church.

Christians are also radically personalist: No response to God in faith has value unless it comes out of a deeply personal decision, conviction and choice. If we basically follow the crowd—any crowd—we can be sure of one thing: We are not following Christ.

The choice to be a Christian is not a choice either to deify or to abdicate the responsibility of personal decision, any more than it is a choice to be a loner or to lose oneself in a crowd. To be a Christian means that we decide—in a deep, personal, intellectual and faith-inspired judgment—to accept Jesus Christ as the Way, the Truth and the Life. It means that we deeply decide to be guided, for the rest of our lives and in all our decisions and choices, by what he taught and did on earth (revelation), by what he teaches and does on earth today in his Church (redeemed culture), by what he inspires and moves us to do within our hearts (redeemed personalism).

To accept Jesus as Savior means to decide to base the rest of our lives on relationship—that is, on *interaction*—with Jesus Christ as the Way, the Truth and the Life: to accept him as our Guide, Teacher and Savior.

Jesus is the Way: He is the Guide who shows us how to live, who gives the directions which preserve our choices from deviation and destructiveness.

Jesus is the Truth: He is the Teacher who saves our perceptions from distortion and falsehood, who gives us knowledge, understanding and wisdom.

Jesus is the Life: He is the empowering Savior who delivers our existence from meaninglessness and diminishment, who heals us and makes us whole, who motivates us and calls us forth, who lifts us up to the level of God's own life.

We embrace Jesus as the constant influence in our lives that we cannot do without. This decision is the pickaxe which breaks up the beaten path of culture and allows the words of God to penetrate.

If we have not yet made the decision to base our whole lives on interaction with the person of Jesus

Christ—if we have not made it as adults: deeply, consciously and radically—it is time to think about it now. Until we have really—that is, effectively—done so, the words of Christ will only rarely penetrate our hearts.

Summary

Theme
Allegiance to culture—to the goals, attitudes and values of this world—will block the words of Christ from entering our hearts.

Goal
To make a deep, conscious, adult, explicit decision to base the rest of our lives on interaction with Jesus Christ as the Way, the Truth and the Life.

Key Thoughts

The Seed That Falls on the Path
   • Whenever the Word of God falls on the hard-beaten path of our cultural conditioning, it just never penetrates.
   • It is not heard and rejected, which would imply understanding and conscious choice; it is simply thrown out before it even has a chance to confront our conscious minds.
   • If anyone, even God himself, says something to us which doesn't match our direction in life at all, or fit into the system of attitudes and values we take for granted, we simply never hear it.

Taking a Pickaxe to the Beaten Path
   • The first condition on our part for entering the Kingdom of God, for accepting Christ's reign over our hearts, is to declare ourselves emancipated from our culture. We have to take a pickaxe to the beaten path.
   • Like the People of Israel, we have to leave the

security of our slavery behind and come out of Egypt. We can allow nothing to determine our lives except the will and the teaching of Jesus Christ.

• Sometime in our lives, and before we can claim to be serious Christians, we have to face the question of which light we will guide our lives by. This is the first, most basic and most radical choice of our Christian existence.

The Meaning of Evangelization

• "[Evangelization] is a question not only of preaching the Gospel in ever wider geographic areas or to ever greater numbers of people, but also of affecting and as it were upsetting, through the power of the Gospel, mankind's criteria of judgment, determining values, points of interest, lines of thought, sources of inspiration and models of life, which are in contrast with the Word of God and the plan of salvation...."

• We cannot truly "hear" what Jesus is saying unless we are willing to go down to the foundation and rebuild our value system from the ground up.

The 'Decision for Christ'

• A Christian break with culture consists essentially in a radical act of accepting Jesus Christ as Savior.

• To accept Jesus Christ as Savior means to make an act of faith that his way is the right way.

• That decision alone is an act of breaking with every culture in the world. It is the choice of a way of life directed from above and directed toward a fulfillment beyond this world. It is a choice of emancipation (though not of rejection or separation) from human culture as such.

What It Means to Be a Christian

• To be a *Christian* does not mean that we cut off either the opinions and wisdom of others or (above all!) the light of our own interior perception.

• To be a Christian means that we decide—in a deep, personal, intellectual and faith-inspired judgment— to accept Jesus Christ as the Way, the Truth and the Life. It means that we deeply decide to be guided, for the rest of our lives and in all our decisions and choices, by what he taught and did on earth, by what he teaches and does on earth today in his Church, by what he inspires and moves us to do within our hearts.

> • To accept Jesus as Savior means to decide to base the rest of our lives on relationship—that is, on *interaction*—with Jesus Christ as the Way, the Truth and the Life: to accept him as our Guide, Teacher and Savior.

Questions for Reflection and Discussion

(If you cannot answer any of the questions below, acknowledge that and then ask how you *could* do what the question asks.)

1. Have I decided as an adult to base my whole life on relationship with Jesus Christ? When did I decide to do this? What led me to it?

2. In what concrete ways do I interact with Jesus?
   - As Savior? As teacher? As leader? As friend?
   - With his mind?
   - With the example he gave on earth?
   - In response to his action in me now?

3. In what concrete ways have I "broken" with this world (with my culture) regarding:
   - Security and material provisions?
   - Family ties and social obligations?
   - Comfort, home and shelter?
   - Status and prestige?
   - Anything else?

4. What can I do now to make my relationship (interaction) with Christ more a part of my daily life?

The Seed That Falls on Rocky Ground

Letting the Word Take Root Through Choices

Preaching a sermon is like throwing gravel on a turtle's back: Even if your words make an impact, very few are liable to stick.

The reason is simple: By the time most people leave the church they have forgotten what the sermon was about. And they never think of it again. They get into the car, turn on the radio or start a conversation with the family, go home and read the funny papers, have Sunday dinner and take up their work again on Monday. The sermon never takes root.

Our Lord says the same about his words.

> "Part of [the seed] fell on rocky ground, where it had little soil. It sprouted at once since the soil had no depth, but when the sun rose and scorched it, it began to wither for lack of roots." (Matthew 13:5-6)

When I left my hometown to enter the novitiate and religious life, I thought back on the sermons I had heard in my parish church while I was growing up. With a shock I realized that I could not remember a single one of them! The only words I could explicitly recall were two jokes the pastor had told!

Later—many years later—I realized that many, many ideas from those sermons had stuck. I couldn't remember them explicitly, but I had definite attitudes and assumptions about religion—some true, some distorted—and these had to have been formed in church. I knew that certain Gospel passages said particular things to me, and those interpretations had to have come through sermons.

Still it is true to say that the words of Jesus never bore the fruit that they could have as I was growing up. And the reason is simple: I never thought about them.

A sermon can't change anyone's life. It is what we *do in response* to a sermon that changes our lives. No words spoken by another person have a determining effect on us until we integrate them into our thinking and choosing, until we make them a part of ourselves.

Our Lord said,

"If you live in me,
and my words *stay part of you*
you may ask what you will—
it will be done for you." (John 15:7, emphasis added)

Another translation for "stay part of you" is "remain in you" or "abide in you" or "live on in you." Christ's words must "live in us" or "abide in us" the way he himself—with the Father and the Spirit—abides in us (see John 14:16-23; 15:4-8, 26). This is a union which is living, active, productive; a union which bears fruit in attitudes, choices and deeds.

Letting Thoughts Take Root

Words don't become part of us—nor do attitudes and values—until we translate them into *choices*. When a "word is made flesh" in choices and action, then it is a part of our incarnate, human reality on this earth. Then it is part of us.

This usually takes time. We don't normally hear a word or listen to an idea and then go right out and put it into practice. We need to think about it, weigh the pros and cons of it, visualize what practical effects it might have on our lives. We need to imagine how that idea could be "made flesh" in the concrete circumstances of our particular situation, what steps we would have to take in order to put it into practice, what other choices would be necessary before we could bring it to realization.

In other words, we have to think about the idea until it takes root. And the idea doesn't take root until it gets down to the level of practical choices, choices that affect our living.

This is why the words of Jesus do not bear the fruit in our lives that they ought to bear: They don't get down to the level of choice. We don't think about them long enough to let them take root.

Converting Words Into Power

Jesus tells us that his words are like seeds. Seeds don't yield instant results. They have to enter into the soil, stay there long enough to take root, then be watered and encouraged to grow. They have to find a receptive environment.

> "The seed that fell on patches of rock is the man who hears the message and at first receives it with joy. But he has no roots, so he lasts only for a time. When some setback or persecution involving the message occurs, he soon falters." (Matthew 13:20-21)

Superficial people make superficial responses. And superficial responses have no power. They are not real responses at all, but illusions. They are the reactions of the moment. We may be "turned on" by an idea as we listen. We nod assent to something said in a sermon. We think we believe it but, in reality, we neither believe nor accept any idea—especially those contained in the Word of God—until we decide to put it into practice.

Words of Life

The words of Jesus are not meant just to "enlighten" us in the sense of increasing our abstract, speculative knowledge. They are meant to enlighten our *path*, to fill us with a truth that excites our love, to give us that light which is also life. The Word of God is a light that empowers (see John 1:1-12).

If we listen to God's Word passively, with our hearts not geared to action, we cannot understand it. We are listening to a call to life as if it were a comment on the scenery.

We do this in other areas of life—we agree with all sorts of ideas in theory until we see what they call for in practice:

"Do you like that car?"
"Yes, very much."
"Would you like to have one like it?"
"Sure."
"Do you want to buy it?"

Now we get down to reality.

Until we start looking at something in terms of practical response, in terms of making a choice about it which affects our lives, we don't really look—we just glance. But when it comes to choices, we begin examining the pros and cons; we do a "cost-benefit analysis" in which we measure advantages against cost. When we do this, we begin to get in touch with just how much we do or do not desire what we say we want, how much we really do believe in all that we have been nodding assent to.

It is the same with Jesus Christ. We don't know how much his words mean to us until we begin to take them for real. How do we do this?

A Decision to Read and Think

There is a very simple way. Sometimes it goes by names that scare us off, esoteric names. But its reality is simple. It amounts to making a very simple decision to start reading and thinking about Scripture.

I purposely did not say, "praying over Scripture." Many people feel they do not know how to pray. Many more are convinced they do not know how to "pray over Scripture." So let's just forget about "prayer."

30

Let's say instead that we will decide to do one simple thing: We will commit ourselves to *read something in Scripture every day and to think about it until* (*until* is the key word here) *we come to some decision that affects our lives.*

This is a method that cannot fail. This is also what we mean by "praying over Scripture." At least, it is one way to pray over Scripture. Just read and start thinking. And think until you are able to see something you can make a decision about. Then make the decision. That is praying over Scripture.

It is also Christian discipleship.

Discipleship: Learning Through Decisions

You don't need to understand everything you read. You don't have to know just exactly what Jesus meant in this statement or that—although it might be interesting to find out. All you have to do is find something in the passage you have read which suggests to you some practical decision you can make that will improve your life. Then make that decision. Once you do, the Word has taken root. You are letting it live in you.

You have begun to learn with your heart as well as your mind, and that is discipleship. You are experiencing the Word as having power: as taking root and beginning to bear fruit in your life. The results may not be very impressive at first, but beginnings usually are not. (Did you ever listen to someone learning to play the piano?)

As time goes on, you may be led every once in a while to make a great decision—something radical and fantastic, something that transforms your whole life. (Such transformation can also happen gradually, almost without your knowing it. You only realize it when you look back later.)

But in your ordinary, daily prayer you don't have to go for the "big play." All you have to insist on is forward motion. Just make decisions. It doesn't matter how small or insignificant they appear, so long as you make them and try to live up to them. Over a period of time they will add up. You will be letting our Lord's words take root in

31

your life. And once they take root, no telling what fruit they will bear.

Discipleship is an unpredictable formula: "Great things happen when God mixes with man!"

A Hands-on Experience

Learning is doing. So let's give you time to practice what I preach!

Confront: You have already read a passage of Scripture while you were reading this chapter. You heard Jesus saying that sometimes his words don't bear fruit because they don't get deep enough in us to take root. How are you going to respond to that?

Think: Get down to the concrete. Ask what you could realistically do to begin some serious reflection on the words of Christ. What kind of decision can you make that you can actually live up to? Put that decision into time and place: "When can I do it? Where? For how long? When do I want to begin?"

Decide: Will I actually do this? Why? (Or why not?) How do I feel about this decision now that I have made it?

A Suggestion You Can't Refuse

I hope you took time to go through the process above and make your decision before continuing to read this. But if you did not, or if you were unable to come to a decision, I have a suggestion! I am encouraged to make it because this suggestion is about the only thing I have ever preached that I have seen people respond to in action.

It is a very simple suggestion: *Get a copy of the Bible. Put it on top of your pillow. Tell God you will never go to sleep without reading one line.*

This may not seem to be much of a decision to make in response to Jesus Christ. But, as I said above, it is the only one I have ever preached which seems to work. The strong point of this suggestion is that it asks so little. One can hardly find an excuse for not reading *one line* of the

Scriptures before going to bed.

Being an author myself of sorts, I believe I know the first question Jesus is going to ask when we get to heaven: "Did you read my book?"

We may begin to stammer, "Lord, that was a pretty thick book. And, you know, life in the 20th century was pitched pretty fast. It was just hard to get time for reading..."

"You couldn't read *one line a night*?"

How will we answer that?

The Naaman Syndrome

The weak point of this suggestion would appear to be that, asking very little, it also gives very little. What good can you gather out of reading one line of Scripture a night?

In the Old Testament a man named Naaman had a similar problem. He had gone to the prophet Elisha to be cured of his leprosy, and the prophet just sent him out a message: "Go and wash seven times in the Jordan, and your flesh will heal." Naaman went away angry, saying, "I thought that the man of God would surely come out and stand there to invoke the LORD his God, and would move his hand over the spot, and thus cure the leprosy. Are not the rivers of Damascus...better than all the waters of Israel? Could I not wash in them and be cleansed?"

Naaman was about to go back home when his servants came up and reasoned with him, "If the prophet had told you to do something extraordinary, would you not have done it? All the more now, since he just said to you, 'Wash and be clean,' you ought to do as he said." So Naaman went and washed, and he was healed (see 2 Kings 5:1-19).

Things don't have to be complex and difficult to be effective. The fact is that anyone who reads even a line of Scripture a night before bed (and why not read another line before getting up in the morning?) is starting and ending the day with a word from Jesus Christ. This is probably more than most of us are doing right now.

Experience has shown that what will actually happen is this: If we pledge to read one line a night, most nights we will read a paragraph—or enough of a passage to give us a complete thought. Most nights, therefore, we will read more than one line.

We must not hold ourselves to this, however, because many nights we will be so tired, or so out of the mood for responding to anything, that the mere thought of reading even a single paragraph would be enough to stop us. But everyone can read one line a night—every night of the year.

If we commit ourselves to this, we will find that in a very short time we have read an entire Gospel, even the whole of the New Testament. (I suggest that you start with the Gospel of Matthew and just keep going. After the four Gospels, you might want to take up the Old Testament— or go on to the Acts of the Apostles and letters of St. Paul.)

A Geographical Detail

I have one final practical suggestion: Keep the Bible on your pillow. Don't put it on the living room table, or even on a table by your bed. If you do that, some night you will forget to pick it up, and no telling when you will remember again. But if you keep the Bible on your pillow, you cannot go to sleep without picking it up. Then read your line, or as much as you feel like reading, and *put the Bible on the floor*—preferably on top of your shoes! That way you can't get up in the morning without picking it up again. When you do, read another line and put the Bible back on your pillow.

This suggestion might sound ridiculously simple and detailed. All I can say in answer is what I have already said: Nothing else that I have ever preached has worked as well as this one suggestion. This is the only thing I have ever proposed that people actually go out and do. Some have told me a year or more later, "Hey, you remember that idea about putting the Bible on your pillow? Well, I did that, and I've been reading Scripture ever since!"

I once gave a parish mission in Memphis,

34

Tennessee. At a youth meeting after the main talk I asked the students to tell me who Jesus Christ was to them. One girl, a senior in high school, gave an answer that took my breath away. I said to her, "You never heard that in school. Where did you learn that?"

She said, "Three years ago, when I was a freshman, you gave a talk in our high school. You said to put the Bible on your pillow and read one line a night. I have read a chapter of the Bible every night since then."

That's letting the seed take root!

Summary

Theme

To be effective in our lives, Christ's words must take root in us. This means they must get down to the level of decisions and choices.

Goal

To make a decision to read at least one line from the Scriptures every night before going to sleep and every morning upon waking up.

Key Thoughts

Introduction
    • A sermon can't change anyone's life. It is what we *do in response* to a sermon that changes our lives.

Letting Thoughts Take Root
    • Words don't become part of us—nor do attitudes and values—until we translate them into choices.
    • When an idea strikes us, we have to think about it until it takes root. And the idea doesn't take root until it gets down to the level of practical choices, choices that affect our living.

Words of Life
    • If we listen to God's Word passively, with our

hearts not geared to action, we cannot understand it. We are listening to a call to life as if it were a comment on the scenery.

A Decision to Read and Think
• Let's say that we will decide to do one simple thing: We will commit ourselves to *read something in Scripture every day and to think about it <u>until</u>* (*until* is the key word here) *we come to some decision that affects our lives.*

'A Suggestion You Can't Refuse'
• *Get a copy of the Bible. Put it on top of your pillow. Tell God you will never go to sleep without reading one line.*

• One can hardly find an excuse for not reading *one line* of the Scriptures before going to bed.

The Naaman Syndrome
• Things don't have to be complex and difficult to be effective. The fact is that anyone who reads even a line of Scripture a night before bed (and why not read another line before getting up in the morning?) is starting and ending the day with a word from Jesus Christ.

• Experience has shown that what will actually happen is that, if we pledge to read one line a night, most nights we will read a paragraph—or enough of a passage to give us a complete thought.

Questions for Reflection and Discussion

1. How much do I think about sermons I hear? About the Scripture read in church, or that I read myself? When do I do this? Where?

2. When is the last time I thought about Scripture (or a sermon) until I made a choice? What was the choice?

3. If I chose to do so, when could I pray over Scripture every day? For how long? Where could I do this?

4. What excuse do I have not to put the Bible on my pillow and read one line a night? Could I do even more than this? (Would I persevere in it if I decided to do more?) Will I do it? Why?

4.

The Seed That Falls Among Thorns
Weeding Out Competing Desires

It is well and good to say, "Pray over Scripture." The fact is that few ever begin, and of those who do, most do not keep it up very long. I believe there are two reasons for this.

The first reason is that many people have not in fact decided—not in a real way—to base the rest of their lives on relationship (that is, on interaction) with Jesus Christ. Jesus is someone they feel no need to interact with daily, because their daily lives are not really based on him. This makes reflecting on his words something optional—an extra, something it would be nice to do but which is not really a necessary part of life. And in this busy world there is small time for extras.

Married couples are an example of people who have chosen to base their lives on relationship with each other. They *have* to communicate, because if they do not, life together becomes impossible. When Jesus Christ is as much a part of our lives as a husband or a wife, then we will communicate seriously with him. And we will persevere in it.

The second reason that few people follow through on Scriptural prayer is that many, once they have begun to pray, hold back from making the *choices* their prayer presents to them. Or they pray in such a way that they don't really look for choices to make. Naturally, anyone whose prayer is leading nowhere will soon abandon it.

Why Prayer Is Barren

Jesus addresses this phenomenon in the Parable of the Sower:

> "Again, part of the seed fell among thorns, which grew up and choked it....What was sown among briers is the man who hears the message, but then worldly anxiety and the lure of money choke it off. Such a one produces no yield." (Matthew 13:7, 22)

What our Lord does here is give the reason why our reflection on Scripture stays barren: Scriptural prayer that doesn't lead to choices "produces no yield." And it doesn't lead to choices, he says, because "worldly anxiety and the lure of money choke it off." We stop praying because "nothing happens"—our prayer doesn't result in action. But it is the very fear of taking action which keeps us from praying well.

This process is not as obvious as it might sound. I believe it is rather uncommon for anyone to consciously face a choice in prayer and then turn away from it. It happens, of course, but when it does it gives us something to pray about later on! The real danger, and the thing that makes us abandon prayer altogether, is the choice we manage *not* to confront at all.

We can choke to death the seeds of life that God is planting in our hearts and not even face the fact that we are doing so. There is a kind of "subliminal perception" in the spiritual life which must be reckoned with. Our minds can see a threatening idea coming before it ever gets into consciousness. And if we don't want that idea to confront us, to disturb our conscience, we can keep it from ever reaching the level of conscious perception. We can do this without even being aware of it.

We are like people who can hear a train approaching long before it comes into sight. And if we do not want to face the question of boarding or not boarding that train, we can pull a switch in our minds and shunt it off onto a sidetrack before it ever reaches the station.

We can read for years the Gospel commandment to love our neighbors as ourselves—and still disassociate ourselves psychologically from the needs of other races, other nationalities, the poor, the Third World countries. We can do this without it ever entering our minds that we are violating a fundamental principle of our religion.

Time and again I have heard people give as a reason for not attending a retreat, not going to church on Sunday, not reading Scripture or spending some time each day in prayer, the same excuses that the people in the Gospel gave for not accepting the man's invitation to the banquet: "I can't take time off from work." "There is too much to do around the house." "I have to be with my family."

> "But they began to excuse themselves, one and all. The first one said to the servant, 'I have bought some land and must go out and inspect it. Please excuse me.' Another said, 'I have bought five yoke of oxen and I am going out to test them. Please excuse me.' A third said, 'I am newly married and so I cannot come.'" (Luke 14:18-20)

What Are Our Priorities?

"We are going to the cabin that weekend." "I have to work on my car." "It's my wife's birthday." "There is no one to stay with the kids." "I need to have my hair done." "That is the only time I have to shop."

Of course obligations—whether family, social or business—take priority over extra spiritual devotions. Anyone who *really* neglected husband, wife or children in order to go on a retreat, attend daily Mass or take part in a prayer group would be making a big mistake—and would be guilty as well of false judgment in the spiritual life.

But most of the excuses one runs into are not real obligations. Or, if they are, they could be handled in such a way that they would not conflict with opportunities for spiritual growth. The problem comes when we use family, business and social commitments as excuses for not doing what we really need to do in order to live an authentically

Christian spiritual life. On this point Jesus is clear: Nothing on earth is so important that it should keep us from living a life of conscious relationship with God, a life that allows us to keep growing in knowledge and love of Jesus Christ and in ever-deepening response to his Gospel.

Jesus says:

> "Stop worrying, then, over questions like, 'What are we to eat, or what are we to drink, or what are we to wear?' The unbelievers are always running after these things. Your heavenly Father knows all that you need. Seek first his kingship over you, his way of holiness, and all these things will be given you besides."
>
> (Matthew 6:31-33)

When we give top priority to the needs and obligations of our life on earth—letting our response to the gospel take second place to family ties, social connections, business opportunities and civic involvement—we are not conscious of deliberately going against the teaching of Jesus Christ. This is because, in all but the most obvious examples, our minds are able to block out any word, teaching or thought which calls into question our priorities or anything to which we are really attached.

Pontius Pilate was ready to free Jesus until he realized what this might cost him; then he just broke off the conversation (see John 19:12-16). We read in the Acts of the Apostles that both in Philippi and in Ephesus Paul was persecuted because his preaching was bad for business (see Acts 16:16-24; 19:23-40). The Roman governor Felix was receptive to Paul's message until he saw his sexual conduct being called into question; then he became frightened and said, "That's enough for now! You can go. I'll send for you again when I find the time" (Acts 24:25).

We do exactly the same thing. We don't have to send anyone away—we just discontinue a certain line of thought, put down a book that is getting to us, or stop going to church. Sometimes we are not even conscious of the reason why we have turned away from the Word that was addressing our hearts.

This is why it is so important for us to be aware of those forces in our hearts—desires, ambitions, attachments, fears, compulsions, appetites—which may be threatened by God's Word and may be choking off its message before it even confronts our power of conscious choice. We have to make a conscious effort to grow in purity—in single-mindedness—of heart because the clarity of our spiritual vision depends on the focus of our hearts. The values our hearts are set on determine what other values we allow to confront our conscious minds.

Loss of Taste for the Things of God

This is true not just in the area of scriptural prayer and reflection on the Gospels. The priority we give to the things of this world does not just block our spiritual growth by preventing us from being receptive to the written and spoken Word of God. It also can cause us to lose our taste for religion itsef—and we will not even know the reason why.

As a chaplain for students, first in high school and later on a college campus, I used to watch young people turning away from religion or even from belief in God. The reasons they gave were seldom, in my opinion, the true ones. On the conscious level they offered intellectual arguments against the existence of God, or spoke of how "meaningless" the rituals of worship had become for them. Sometimes they accused the Church (the believing community) of "hypocrisy."

At the same time, they had already begun to act in ways contrary to Christian morality—usually with rationalizations which kept them from admitting, even to themselves, that this was sin.

No one can live a contradiction very long. When the conduct one embraces is incompatible with the faith one professes, something has to give. If one is unable to admit sin, to accept weakness and moral struggle, and to ask repeatedly for forgiveness until the problem is resolved, the obvious alternative is to rationalize.

But rationalization only affects the head; the heart still feels the contradiction. Then every celebration of worship and faith becomes meaningless, even repugnant. How can one celebrate the basic contradiction of one's life?

Anyone who has broken with the ideals of the Christian community in practice—and is refusing to admit it with honesty and accept it with humility—is no longer comfortable with the community. This is not because the community is in fact judgmental or rejecting (the community may not even know how a person is behaving), but because when our conduct is incompatible with the community's belief, we ourselves feel alienated in our hearts.

When sin is admitted as sin, this sense of alienation does not exist—or is not as intense. To admit sin means to reject it, at least on the level of ideals. It is to long for deliverance, to keep oneself open for deliverance, to hope for deliverance even if one knows one is not yet ready to accept it.

Anyone in this condition of soul can identify very deeply with the Christian message. The Word is addressed to sinners. The Good News of Christ is that the sinful are called to be saints! Jesus said, "People who are in good health do not need a doctor; sick people do....I have come to call, not the self-righteous, but sinners" (Matthew 9:12-13).

That is why both sinners and saints are comfortable with Jesus, and why both are comfortable in the Church. Only those who are unable to admit their sin—or to respond even to the dream of being a saint—feel alienated.

Alienation: A Sign of Resistance

Many people feel alienated from the Church today in greater or lesser degree: Some find the Church too conservative, some find her too liberal; others feel alienated because the preaching turns them off or the liturgy fails to turn them on. Some still cling to resentments from the past. Alienation from the Church, however, is not caused by what other people do or do not do. Alienation is an experience of ourselves. Usually it is a sign of some resistance within us to the Spirit moving our hearts.

Since we are not devoted to facing ourselves, this sense of alienation might translate, on the conscious level, into criticism of liturgy or preaching, or into accusations of hypocrisy and coldness on the part of the congregation. And, in fact, when someone is resisting the Word of God, everything experienced in church may make a negative impression: The experience of being "turned off" by worship services is real. (All the faults that are criticized may be real also!) The true source of these perceptions, however, and the reason why the community's self-expression affects the person as it does, is the unrecognized conflict within the person's own heart: *Quidquid recipitur, secundum modum recipientis recipitur*. The Word is falling among thorns.

Our Lord speaks as if it were almost a foregone conclusion that in competition with the values of this world his Word will lose out: "Part of the seed fell among thorns, which grew up and choked it." Is his Word, then, such a fragile thing?

Until it has taken root deeply enough in a person's heart, yes, it is. God can always speak with power, of course. There are plenty of instances in history of God's simply smiting the heart with his grace—knocking St. Paul down on the road to Damascus, for example (see Acts 9: 1-19). But ordinarily God is so careful not to violate our freedom that if our hearts are not relatively pure, his Word cannot even begin to flourish there.

This is another way of saying that the Word of God can be choked out by thorns, and if we want the words of Jesus to flourish in our hearts, we have to weed the garden. That is why "purification of heart" is a necessary exercise of the Christian life. It is a prerequisite for progress in the life of grace.

45

What Is 'Purification of Heart'?

The phrase *pure of heart* is sometimes translated "single-hearted." To be pure is to be unmixed. Anything which keeps us from loving the Lord, our God, with undivided love—with our whole heart, whole soul and whole strength—diminishes purity of heart. It is a weed to be rooted out.

A weed is anything that is in competition with God. A thorn is anything which chokes off the expansion of his Word into our practical lives. "Purification of heart" is the process by which we root out of our lives the weeds and the thorns—anything, that is, which keeps us from clearly hearing the Word of God and responding to it with perfect freedom.

It isn't just sin that we have to root out. The examples Jesus mentions in his parable—"worldly anxiety and the lure of money"—are simply values in competition with God. Any human value which has such an attraction for us, such a hold on our hearts, that we are tempted to compromise on loyalty to God in order to enjoy it is a thorn.

Purity of heart is not diminished by the fact that we love something or someone and are strongly attracted to human goodness and beauty. The ideal of Christianity, of the graced life, is to be *fully human and fully divine*. If we do not have complete human appreciation for human values, we are not fully human.

It is not appreciation or enjoyment of created values as such that diminishes purity of heart; it is dividedness on the level of the will. It is possible to have desire for something—even strong desire—and at the same time be so single-heartedly committed to the will of God that the desire is not a temptation. On the level of the will—that is, on the practical level of actual decision and choice—there may not be the slightest question of satisfying one's desire in any way that is sinful or holds us back from total response to the will of God. In such a case the desire is not in competition with God. It is not a weed or a bramble and does not choke off the Word.

We are not talking here about unresisted "bad" thoughts, about worldly daydreams or deliberate fantasies and longings for what is incompatible with grace. These *do* diminish purity of heart. We are saying there is no conflict between undivided love for God and deep appreciation of the goodness of created persons and things. God can be loved in his creatures.

Dividedness of heart, then, is measured not by the strength of our love for or attraction to created things, but by the wholeheartedness of our will's adhesion to God. The stronger our commitment to God, the more authentic appreciation for the things of this world we can afford to have without the danger of lessened loyalty to God. But if our attraction to the values of this world draws us away from God in any way, or disturbs the freedom of our response to the Gospel, we are dealing with the problem of the thorns.

How do we deal with this problem? That is the topic of our next chapter.

Summary

Theme
Any attachment of our hearts to the things of this world can prevent us from hearing and understanding the Word of God.

Goal
To determine to seek "purity of heart"—that is, single-minded adhesion to the will of God in all our desires.

Key Thoughts

Introduction

• The first reason why many people do not persevere in praying over Scripture is that they have not in fact decided to base the rest of their lives on relationship with Jesus Christ.

 • The second reason is that many people, once they have begun to pray, hold back from making the *choices* their prayer presents to them. Or they pray in such a way that they don't really look for choices to make.

Why Prayer Is Barren

 • Our reflection on Scripture stays barren, doesn't lead to choices, because "worldly anxiety and the lure of money choke it off."

 • We stop praying because "nothing happens"—our prayer doesn't result in action. But it is the very fear of taking action which keeps us from praying well.

 • The real danger, and the thing that makes us abandon prayer altogether, is the choice we manage *not* to confront at all.

 • There is a kind of "subliminal perception" in the spiritual life which must be reckoned with. Our minds can see a threatening idea coming. And if we don't want that idea to confront us, we can keep it from ever reaching the level of conscious perception without even being aware of it.

What Are Our Priorities?

 • When we give top priority to the needs and obligations of our life on earth—letting our response to the gospel take second place—we are not conscious of deliberately going against the teaching of Jesus Christ.

 • This is why it is so important for us to be aware of those forces in our hearts—desires, ambitions, attachments, fears, compulsions, appetites—which may be threatened by God's Word and may be choking off its message before it ever confronts our power of conscious choice.

 • We have to make a conscious effort to grow in purity—in single-mindedness—of heart because the clarity of our spiritual vision depends on the focus of our hearts.

Loss of Taste for the Things of God

 • The priority we give to the things of this world can

cause us to lose our taste for religion itself—and we will not even know the reason why.

• Anyone who has broken with the ideals of the Christian community in practice and is refusing to admit it is no longer comfortable with the community. When our conduct is incompatible with the community's belief, we ourselves feel alienated in our hearts.

Alienation: A Sign of Resistance

• Alienation from the Church is not caused by what other people do or do not do. Alienation is an experience of ourselves. Usually it is a sign of some resistance within us to the Spirit moving our hearts.

• Ordinarily God is so careful not to violate our freedom that if our hearts are not relatively pure, his Word cannot even begin to flourish there.

• That is why "purification of heart" is a necessary exercise of the Christian life. It is a prerequisite condition for progress in the life of grace.

What Is 'Purification of Heart'?

• To be pure is to be unmixed. Anything which keeps us from loving the Lord, our God, with undivided love diminishes purity of heart. It is a weed to be rooted out.

• "Purification of heart" is the process by which we root out of our lives anything which keeps us from clearly hearing the Word of God and responding to it with perfect freedom.

• It isn't just sin that we have to root out, but any human value which has such an attraction for us that we are tempted to compromise on loyalty to God in order to enjoy it.

• It is not appreciation or enjoyment of created values as such that diminishes purity of heart; it is dividedness on the level of the will.

• Dividedness of heart is measured, not by the strength of our love for or attraction to created things, but by the firmness of our will's adhesion to God.

Questions for Reflection and Discussion

1. If I have not been able to persevere in praying over Scripture, do I think the reason might be:
   - that I have never deeply decided—in a real way—to base my day-to-day life on relationship (interaction) with Jesus Christ?
   - that my prayer has not led to choices and is therefore sterile?

2. Can I identify—in retrospect—any experience in my life of being blind to truth or deaf to God's Word because of something I was attached to, did not want to change in my life?

3. Can I recall any instance of beginning to see some value or teaching of Jesus once my attachment to something was broken—for example, because I lost it anyway?

4. What is "purification of heart"? Have I experienced the need for this? How?

5.

The Seed Choked by Briers
Putting 'Human' Attachment to Death

Purification of heart and increased spiritual perception go together. Without a certain purity of heart, we will not even see the choices to which we are called by the Word of God. If we do not see them, we will not make them, and our reflection on Scripture will be sterile. Prophetic insights, therefore, come through purification; the discoveries of discipleship are dependent on continual conversion.

When the thorns of competing desire choke off the Word of God in our hearts, they first obscure its meaning. Like the Philistines who blinded Samson before they put him to work (see Judges 16:21), our desires have to blind us before they can thoroughly enslave us. And that is the greatest danger of unevaluated desires: They are able to take away our sight so that we are not even aware of what Christ calls us to be. We think we are responding to him, directing our lives by his words. But like a driver falling asleep at the wheel, we begin to veer off course without even realizing it.

Comfort is like a warm bath: It draws our attention to our surface experience of pleasure and puts our soul to sleep. All attachment to a lower, more comfortable level of life keeps us from even perceiving higher ideals. If we restrict our desires to mediocrity, our vision will be limited to the mediocre also. Then Jesus himself can call us to "lift up our eyes," and we will not even recognize the radicalness of his words. (That may be the reason why the Eucharistic celebration invites us instead: "Lift up your hearts"!)

What we are saying here is that all vision depends on focus. Spiritual vision depends on the focus of our hearts. The focus of the heart determines the focus of the intellect: When our desires are fixed on immediate gratification we suffer a myopia of the mind. If we want to understand the Word of God, then, we have to refocus our desires.

How do we do this? In the vocabulary of spiritual writers, the classic word for this process of refocusing is *mortification*.

A New Look at an Old Word

To "mortify" oneself literally means to "put to death" something within oneself. No wonder it sounds negative! And if we take the word at its face value, it would be anti-Christian.

A first principle of Christian spirituality is that we are called to the "fullness of life," both human and divine (see John 10:10). We do not become more divine by making ourselves less human. Nor do we open ourselves more to grace by "killing" (numbing, neutralizing) any part or power of our human nature. The guiding principle for Christians is that in all our thoughts, desires and actions we should, as much as possible, be "fully human and fully divine"—as Jesus himself was.

Here's the paradox: In order to achieve this, we have to "die to ourselves." When Matthew describes Jesus sending out his apostles to preach for the first time, he presents Jesus as saying to them:

> "I have come to set a man at odds with his father, a daughter with her mother, a daughter-in-law with her mother-in-law: in short, to make a man's enemies those of his own household. Whoever loves father or mother, son or daughter, more than me is not worthy of me. He who will not take up his cross and come

after me is not worthy of me. He who seeks only himself brings himself to ruin, whereas he who brings himself to nought for me discovers who he is."

(Matthew 10:35-39)

A more literal translation of this last line is: "He who would save his life will lose it, but whoever loses his life for my sake will find it." Jesus is saying that, in order to accept the gift of higher life which he offers, we have to go against the inertia of human life. Our natural desires and appetites tend to keep us always in the same orbit, to restrict us to the plane of ordinary, human action and ideals. In order to accept the goals and ideals, the principles, attitudes and values taught by Jesus Christ, we have to break out of our ordinary, human orbit, break free of our ordinary, human way of understanding and evaluating things. We have to drop some weight in order to soar.

The desires we are talking about are good; they are human. But they aim no higher than ordinary, human satisfaction and behavior. That is why, in order to accept the divine life and teaching of Jesus, we have to go against them. We have to fight them to be free.

A key point here is that mortification does not focus on overcoming sin. We seek purity of heart not when we turn away from what is evil, but when we fight to free ourselves from bondage to what is good. The goal of Christian mortification is not to die to all that keeps us from being normally human. It is to die to all that keeps us from being "supernormally" divine. We struggle to free ourselves from all that restricts us to our natural, human orbit, because the gospel calls us to live on the level of God's own divine life.

To be able to see, to hear, to perceive, to accept the meaning of Christ's words calling us to live on the level of God, we have to be sure we are free to go beyond the human level.

If attachment to human values can blind us even to the difference between good and evil, and obscure a judgment of common moral sense, it goes without saying that the same attachment can blind us even more completely to the radical call of the gospel. The gospel goes beyond common sense. It is addressed to those who do not find it sufficient to be good (see Matthew 19:16-22). Its promises—and therefore its demands—are only intelligible to those who ask from life more than life itself can offer. To really listen to the gospel we have to look beyond our orbit. We have to break the gravitational pull of everything on this earth that can hold us down.

This means that we have to break the hold that good, human values and desires have on us. We have to be sure that we can appreciate all that is good without any of it having the power to hold us back, to influence our spiritual judgment, to obscure our perception, to block our response to the Word of God. This means more than defending ourselves against what is evil. It means taking the offensive even against what is captivatingly good. We do this until we are certain we are free.

Free to Be Divine

St. Paul's theme song is that we should live "according to the Spirit" rather than "according to the flesh." We should "put to death" (mortify) the desires of the flesh in order to live by the Spirit (see Romans 8:12-13).

When Paul speaks of human nature or of the "flesh," he usually passes over in silence—as if it did not exist—any level of human activity which is just natural and good but not necessarily graced. This could lead us to assume that Paul thinks our created natures as such are evil and corrupt, and that no ordinary human action has value unless it is transformed by grace.

But this is not what Paul is trying to say. He is not making any abstract statements about the value of human activities—joys, pleasures, accomplishments—as such. His focus is on what Christians reborn in grace should aim at in their lives. And he exhorts them—and us—to live, not good human lives, but superhuman, supernatural lives as sharers in the divine nature of Christ.

54

When Paul gives examples he usually contrasts the two extremes, the top and the bottom. He presents a choice between surrender to the Spirit and abject slavery to the flesh, between the divine life of Christ and the corruption of human behavior which is sin:

> Put to death whatever in your nature is rooted in earth: fornication, uncleanness, passion, evil desires, and that lust which is idolatry....all the anger and quick temper, the malice, the insults, the foul language. Stop lying to one another.
>
> (Colossians 3:5, 8-9)

These examples of sins—that is, of subhuman behavior to avoid—are not presented in a setting of exhortation to live merely good human lives. St. Paul never speaks of anything but our call to live on the superhuman, divine level of members of the Body of Christ, made one with Christ the Head in the unity of one shared life and activity:

> I became a minister of this church through the commission God gave me to preach among you his word in its fullness, that mystery hidden from ages and generations past but now revealed to his holy ones...the mystery of Christ in you, your hope of glory.
>
> In Christ the fullness of deity resides in bodily form. Yours is a share of this fullness, in him....
>
> Since you have been raised up in company with Christ, set your heart on what pertains to higher realms where Christ is seated at God's right hand. Be intent on things above rather than on things of earth. After all, you have died! Your life is hidden now with Christ in God.
>
> What you have done is put aside your old self with its past deeds and put on a new man, one who grows in knowledge as he is formed anew in the image of his

Creator. (Colossians 1:25-27; 2:9; 3:1-3, 9-10)

Paul is not talking here about converting from sin to good, human behavior. He is talking about living as the Body of Christ on earth—that is, about knowing and willing and loving on the level of Christ himself.

Paul contrasts the life of grace not just with a life of sin, but with any level of human behavior—no matter how good—which is not enlightened by the light of faith, inspired by the love which God pours out in our hearts, strengthened by the indwelling presence of the Holy Spirit. In short, Paul contrasts the life of grace with any level of behavior which is not in actual fact behavior animated by the indwelling presence and power of Jesus Christ himself.

We are the Body of Christ. He lives and acts in us; we live and act "in Christ," in union with him, as co-sharers in his life, cooperators (co-actors) with him in his activity. This is Paul's most constant theme (see, for example, Romans 12:1-8; 1 Corinthians 2:6-16; 12:1-13; Ephesians 1:3-23; 3:14-21; 5:22-32).

This is a level of operation so far above our normal level that we have to become adjusted to it. This calls for a refocusing, first of all, on the level of intellectual understanding and openness. Our minds have to be attuned to receiving inspirations to act on God's level; otherwise, any impulse, movement of heart or thought of acting on the level of Christ's own divine ideals would be thrown out immediately as outlandish and "superhuman."

This adjustment, this new mindset, is accomplished in part by the "emancipation from culture" which takes us off the "beaten path" and lets Christ's Word penetrate our defenses of prejudice and previous assumptions. It is also accomplished through reading and reflecting on the words and example of Christ as presented in Scripture.

But, before we can understand Scripture as we should, there is another line of defense which must be neutralized: the defenses of the heart. These are the defenses set up by our affective attachments and desires. These are the "thorns" Jesus speaks about which choke off the Word because it is a threat to something we cling to, something we fear to lose.

How do we neutralize these defenses?

Breaking Gravitational Pull

The answer is to set out systematically to break the power of anything within us that is in competition with God. We do this by identifying those appetites which threaten our freedom of heart and denying them satisfaction until we are sure that we are free. This is "mortification." It is an active exercise of the spiritual life.

If we experience some appetite, some desire, as able—actually or potentially—to restrict our unreserved response to the gospel, we simply "mortify" that desire. We fast from the satisfaction of that appetite until we know that we are able to do so, that we have achieved mastery over it, that it is no real threat to our freedom of thought and action.

Food, for example, is good. But we don't know how much control food has over us until we have tried to fast. Riches and possessions are also good. We simply don't know, however, whether an attachment to affluence is coloring our perception of the gospel until we verify from deliberate experience and experimentation that we can be content with very little. It is good to have friends and to build strong, human relationships. We don't know how much the opinions of others dominate us, though, until we risk being different. We don't know how dependent we are on the security of job and family until we face the prospect of leaving them

Whenever our self-interest makes us *want* something to be true—our company's ethics, our boss's policies, our family's priorities, the values of our own social group, the opinions of a spouse or friend, the political philosophy of the party which helps us make a living, the religious stance which justifies our personal conduct—we tend to resonate sympathetically with the arguments which make it true. When we "know which side our bread is buttered on," we subconsciously turn the other side face down: We neither see it nor hear it.

To become free to hear we need to get rid of the static. In order to see with the eyes of Christ we have to free ourselves for a while—physically, or in some other real way—from whatever could be obscuring the vision of our minds and enslaving our hearts. To be sure we have broken out of the gravitational field of this world—that we have "left" affectively, in will and desire, all that we are enslavingly attached to—we have to "leave" this world in fact. We have to leave it behind in some real way, just to experience what it is like to be free.

This is the path to freedom taught by God himself. He required Abraham, as a condition for receiving the promise of transcendent fulfillment, to actually leave everything that gave his life meaning here on earth (see Genesis 12:1). Later God put Abraham to the test of sacrificing even the fulfillment of the promise, as Abraham understood it (see Genesis 22). God required the people of Israel actually to leave Egypt, to come out of their place of slavery and follow him through the desert in trust (see Exodus 12—13; 16:2-3; Numbers 14:1-4). He inspired Elijah the prophet not to accept Elisha as his successor until the young man was ready to abandon everything else for his mission (see 1 Kings 19:19-21). Later Jesus made it clear that this was the spirit in which his own disciples must follow him (see Matthew 4:18-22; 8:19-22).

Mortification, then, is not just detachment of heart. It is some real, physical act of detaching oneself from real human values in order to test or to actualize detachment of heart. Mortification consists in doing something. And this is the condition for really hearing the Word of God. It is the price one pays to be a prophet and to bear prophetic witness in the world.

Uniting Words to Action
The true prophets always come out of the desert, for this is where the Word of God is spoken (see Luke 3:2).

Like John the Baptizer, they are dressed in camel's hair and their food is grasshoppers and wild honey (see Matthew 3:4). When our Lord sent his disciples out to preach, he required of them a life-style, a physical way of eating, dressing and providing for themselves which of itself proclaimed the Good News of the Kingdom (see Matthew 10:9-10). Jesus knew that unless the words we preach are first made flesh in our life-style, even we ourselves will not perceive their meaning.

It is one thing to challenge cultural attitudes and values in words, on the level of theory. It is another thing to break with them in action, on the level of real life. Just to *say* things that go contrary to culture is to be nothing but a coffeehouse prophet: Any college student with a folk song and a guitar can do that. It is only in actually *doing* something contrary to cultural attitudes and values that we become free—free enough to see with the eyes of Christ.

Words and action go together. A word is not fully real until it is "made flesh" in action. When it comes to the Word of God, however, we have to add a further clarification: Action frequently *precedes* understanding. The higher God's Word is calling us to rise, the less we will perceive what the Word itself means until we have begun to *act against* those things which are in competition with it.

After the resurrection, it was in the "breaking of the bread" that the disciples' eyes were opened and they recognized Jesus (see Luke 24:30-31). In the same way, it is only in the act of breaking open our hearts, offering up in sacrifice the goals and values of this world in some real way, that our eyes are opened and we are able to see the Lord.

To act against the competition in some positive way by breaking its power over us is called "mortification." It is a stepping-stone to purity of heart. And purity of heart is the counterpart of vision: "Blessed are the pure of heart, for they shall see God."

Those who want the seed of God's Word to flourish in their hearts and bear real fruit in their lives will prepare the ground. They will go to work on the thorns. The decision to make now is, "Where shall I begin?"

The answer might be to begin with the first concrete suggestion your mind spontaneously rejects!

Summary

Theme
A necessary step toward purification of heart is mortification.

Goal
To decide to identify those desires in our hearts which are in competition with God's Word and actively work with God to "put them to death" by acting against them.

Key Thoughts

Introduction

• Prophetic insights come through purification; the discoveries of discipleship are dependent on continual conversion.

• Comfort is like a warm bath: It draws our attention to our surface experience of pleasure and puts our soul to sleep. All attachment to a lower, more comfortable level of life keeps us from even perceiving higher ideals.

A New Look at an Old Word

• To "mortify" oneself literally means to "put to death" something within oneself.

• A first principle of Christian spirituality is that we are called to the "fullness of life," both human and divine.

• We do not become more divine by making ourselves less human. We do not open ourselves more to grace by "killing" (numbing, neutralizing) any part or power of our human nature.

• The guiding principle for Christians is that in all our thoughts, desires and actions we should, as much as possible, be "fully human and fully divine"—as Jesus himself was.

• The paradox is that, in order to achieve this, we have to "die to ourselves." In order to accept the gift of higher life which he offers, we have to go against the inertia of human life.

• Mortification does not focus on overcoming sin. We seek purity of heart not when we turn away from what is evil, but when we fight to free ourselves from bondage to what is good.

• The goal of Christian mortification is to cooperate with God who wishes to free us from all that restricts us to our natural, human orbit, because the gospel calls us to live on the level of God's own divine life.

• To really listen to the gospel we have to look beyond our orbit. We have to break the gravitational pull of everything on this earth that can hold us down.

Breaking Gravitational Pull

• The answer is to set ourselves systematically to break the power of anything within us that is in competition with God's Word.

• We do this by identifying those appetites which threaten our freedom of heart and denying them satisfaction until we are sure that we are free. This is "mortification." It is an active exercise of the spiritual life.

• To become free to hear God's Word we have to free ourselves for a while actually—physically, or in some other real way—from whatever could be obscuring the vision of our minds and enslaving our hearts. We do this by "mortification."

• To be sure we have "left" affectively, in will and desire, all that we are enslavingly attached to, we have to "leave" this world in fact. We have to leave it behind in some real way, just to experience what it is like to be free.

• Mortification, then, is not just detachment of heart. It is some real, physical act of detaching oneself from real human values in order to test or to actualize detachment of heart.

Uniting Words to Action

• When our Lord sent his disciples out to preach, he required of them a life-style which of itself proclaimed the Good News of the Kingdom.

• It is only in actually *doing* something contrary to cultural attitudes and values that we become free—free enough to see with the eyes of Christ.

• The higher God's Word is calling us to rise, the less we will perceive what the Word itself means until we have begun to *act against* those things which are in competition with it.

Questions for Reflection and Discussion

1. How do my emotions respond to the words "mortification" or "mortify yourself"?

2. How is mortification, properly understood, an enhancement of life and not a diminishment?

3. Is the goal of mortification to help us overcome sin? If not, then what does it help us overcome?

4. How does mortification help us to see? What does it help us to see?

6.

The Seed That Doesn't Bear Fruit

Making Decisions, Working Toward Ideals

A constant theme throughout this book has been that people do not let the Word of God, the words of Jesus, actually "take flesh" in their lives—in concrete decisions, choices and actions. And this is what keeps the Word from bearing fruit.

In this chapter we want to force ourselves to get concrete. We want to pull our minds out of the air and focus them on some ground-level reality—on something real in our lives.

Surprisingly enough, I have found that adults are frequently less able to do this than adolescents. I used to end my retreats, both for adults and for teenagers, with this concrete suggestion:

Sit down and write out two things: an *ideal* and a *decision*. The ideal should be a goal, something you want to arrive at, something you are willing to work toward. The decision, however, should be something concrete and practical that will help you come closer to the goal.

The ideal will probably be something you are unable to do, to accomplish at this moment. The decision, however, should be something you can do, some definite action which you can tie down to time and space and which is within your spiritual reach right now. Above all, make your decision concrete!

At the last ceremony of the retreat, I would invite them to put on the altar the papers on which they had written their ideals and decisions. What I found out was that, by and large, the adults could not distinguish between the two: Instead of one ideal and one decision they generally wrote down two ideals—two vague and general resolutions to "do better" in some particular area of life. For example:

Ideal: A better marriage. *Decision*: I will communicate more deeply with my spouse.

Ideal: To be a better parent. *Decision*: I will be more patient with my kids.

Ideal: To know Christ better. *Decision*: I will pray more.

None of these is a real decision. Not one of them can be put immediately into practice without it first being brought down to a more concrete level in time and space. Real decisions to accompany the above ideals would be something like:

Ideal: To communicate better with my spouse. *Decision*: At 5:30 every afternoon, when my spouse and I are both home, the first thing I will do is sit down and listen for 30 minutes.

Ideal: To be more patient with my children. *Decision*: When one of them is getting on my nerves I will go for a walk around the block thinking of all the things I love in that child. Then I will try to handle the situation.

Ideal: To pray more. *Decision*: This Saturday morning I will go to the bookstore and buy a couple of tapes on the spiritual life. I will turn one on each morning when I start my car and listen to it on the way to work.

These are concrete decisions. They are tied down to time and space. They are something you can probably do—or, if not, you will know immediately that you have failed to do what you decided and you can look for a decision more on your real level.

For some reason, teenagers seemed better able to distinguish between general ideals and concrete decisions. One high school boy turned in as his ideal: "To always speak as the Body of Christ on earth." Sublime. His decision was: "No more [expletive] and [expletive]." From the sublime to the real!

Another gave as his goal, "To respect every girl on a date as the Body of Christ himself" (that retreat focused a lot on our reality as Christ's Body on earth). His decision: "Not to do anything with her that I could not do with my sister."

But he put an asterisk after this and added a postscript at the bottom of the page: "Except kissing." His decision was real enough for him to be sure his commitment had limits!

Solo Flight

So in what concrete area will you begin to seek "purification of heart?" In what concrete way will you begin to "mortify" yourself?

Has food got too much of a hold on you? Could you fast once a week? (On what day? How much and when will you eat on that day?)

Too hard? Then how about cutting meat to once a day for a week or so, just to see if you need to eat as affluently as you do?

Your budget has already solved that problem for you? Then try limiting yourself to one helping of something you usually load up on, or refraining from dessert. Or leave the sauce or salt off your food, the sugar out of your coffee, just to see if you really are free to determine for yourself how you will eat.

Food is not your weak point? How about drink? Not a problem drinker? Try giving up alcohol for two weeks, just to study your reactions to it, the difference it does or does not make in your life. Or try keeping to one beer at a meal, two drinks at a party.

Are you addicted to clothes? How many things are there in your closet that you haven't worn in a year? Try giving some of them away. Or put them in a box for a year, and if you find you never need to take them out, then give them away. Try not buying anything new for a specified period of time, just to find out whether you are using new clothes as a crutch.

Here's a good one: Decide that for one week you will never interrupt anyone who is speaking or about to speak. I did this once and found out that in most groups this will keep you totally silent: No one gets the floor in a group conversation except through interrupting. This may reveal to you some interesting things about the need you have to talk and the quality of your conversation.

Try saying "yes" to everything you are asked to do for one day—a week if you are courageous. See whether it kills you.

Are you attached to sleeping too late? Going to bed too late? Try getting up and going to the early-morning Mass for a month, for Advent, for Lent. Is it really impossible? Is it worth the sacrifice? How will you know until you try it?

TV-watching is an obvious attachment. Are you a slave to the tube? See what happens to your family life, your spirits, if you just lock up the set for a week. Or if you decide ahead of time on two or three programs during the week and watch only those. Learn by doing: How can you make the best use, the most life-enriching use of TV?

The same applies to reading material. What do you read? Do you always take the easy way over what might be the more enriching way?

Do you regularly watch TV instead of reading? Do you read only escapist novels? Or do you do some serious reading? (You must do some, or you wouldn't be reading this book!) Try giving a certain amount of time each night—10 minutes, 15 minutes—to reading a spiritual book. Do it for a month. Evaluate the results.

How much of a hold does money have on you? Are you dominated by an insecurity you don't even feel? Do you, in fact—and perhaps without even noticing it—try first and foremost to make sure you have enough set aside to meet your financial needs? Or do you first and foremost express trust in God through your use of money? Try "tithing" for a year, for a couple of months. Take a percentage off the top and give it to charity *before* you meet any other obligations. It doesn't have to be a large percentage. See what you learn through it, what you experience.

Are you really free to express your own mind? Your faith? Do you hide your light under a bushel basket because you are afraid not to blend in with the crowd? Try "mortifying" your fears for a while, just to see what happens. For one day, for a week, make a point of saying whatever you really think about a matter under discussion (not about a person, however, unless it is good!).

When is the last time you actually talked to another person about your religion, your faith, your love for God? When did you last hold back from saying something because you were afraid of sounding religious? Are you sure you are free? Try praying in public a couple of times (grace before meals in a restaurant, for instance) or just out loud with your family. Get your courage together and suggest family prayer for a week, for a special occasion.

Are you a slave to the shortage of time? When is the last time you took off to make a weekend retreat? Have you "always intended" to make the Cursillo, a Marriage Encounter? Mortify your fear, give up some of the time you are sure you do not have. Give a weekend to intensive spiritual growth.

The list could go on indefinitely. But these are enough suggestions to start your mind working. There may be just one more worth suggesting: Is there one idea that keeps coming back to you and that you keep putting out of your mind? Try doing that one.

The seed doesn't bear fruit until it takes root. The seed of God's Word is often choked off by the competition before it even has a chance to get down to the level of choices. So do a little weeding: Clear the ground, get rid of a few things that may be keeping God's Word from bearing fruit in your life. Make room for life and experience the Reign of God.

Summary

Theme
A decision is not real and concrete unless it concerns a particular action in time and space.

Goal
To make some real decision in response to this book.

Key Thoughts

Introduction
　　• An ideal is a goal, something you probably cannot do now but want to arrive at. A decision is some concrete action you are able to do now which will help you come closer to the ideal.
　　(The other thoughts were some concrete suggestions for seeking purification of heart.)

Questions for Reflection and Discussion

1. In what area of my life will I seek purification of heart?

2. Can I specify an *ideal* in this area (a goal I want to arrive at) and a *decision* (a concrete action which is a means for arriving at this goal)? What will they be?

3. Is my decision something concrete, tied down to time and space? Am I actually able to do it right now?

4. How do I feel about having made this decision?

7.

The Seed That Lands on Good Soil

Nurturing the Word in the Garden of Community

When we read the Parable of the Sower, we sometimes focus only on the seeds that do not grow. Our Lord ends, however, rejoicing in the seed that "landed on good soil and yielded grain a hundred- or sixty- or thirtyfold" (Matthew 13:8). What was sown on good soil, he says, is "the man who hears the message and takes it in" (13:23).

We have seen some obstacles to this: enslavement to the "beaten path" of culture; a superficial listening to the Word without the kind of reflection which leads to choices (rocky ground); a binding (and therefore blinding) attachment to the gratifications of "ordinary" human existence (thorns). All of these things restrict us to a lower orbit of life. They keep us from even perceiving and recognizing the heights to which we are called by the Word of God.

Now, however, we ask what prepares us positively to receive the Word. What makes us "good soil"? The answer is *community*.

Seeds grow best in gardens. People who are serious about growing things group their seeds together in a special place: in a field that has been prepared and plowed. When seeds are planted together like this, the environment becomes theirs. The land becomes specifically a place for nurturing seed. It is not a hostile or even a neutral environment; it is a garden.

And this is what Christian community is: an

environment which nurtures the Word of God.

What Makes a Community a Community?

We should be careful not to associate "Christian community" with some particular form of community with which we do or do not feel comfortable. Some people think community means a commune, or a monastery, or a prayer group, or a large body of people animated by enthusiasm and sustained by one another.

A community, however, is just a "common unity." It exists whenever there is a common commitment which is real and is expressed in ways that are evident and credible to all.

A community of love exists whenever two or more people are united in love and communicate this love in a language they all understand and believe.

A faith community exists whenever two or more people are joined in a common commitment to the Word of God and express this commitment to one another in ways that make their faith evident and credible to all. Jesus said, "Where two or three are gathered in my name, there am I in their midst" (Matthew 18:20).

The essential elements of community, then, are these:

1) Two or more people

2) with a common commitment

3) who give expression to this commitment

4) in a "language" (words, symbols, actions, choices, life-style)

5) that all the members understand

6) and that is credible.

The key element in this definition of community is *expression*. A group of people—Christians, for example—who do in fact share a common commitment, but who do not express that commitment in ways that make it recognizable to each other are not a community.

Ten (or two) Christians can live in the same house together and not be a Christian community. A rectory, or a religious house, or a family can be made up entirely of believing, committed Christians and still not be a *Christian* community.

For community to exist, the common commitment of the members must be *expressed*. And it must be expressed in language *all understand*. If all the members give expression to their commitment, but each one does this in symbols, language or choices which the others cannot recognize as an expression of Christian commitment, there is no awareness of unity, no sense of oneness, no community.

Furthermore, the expression of commitment must be *credible*. This means that it must stand out as more than words. Words are too easy to pronounce, their real meaning too easy to ignore. If we say, "We believe in Jesus Christ," others can't know what that means (to us) until they see how we live it out. And we won't know what it means to one another until we see how each one lives it out.

Verbal and Nonverbal Expression

Actions speak louder than words. And silence sometimes speaks louder than actions.

I once spent a year in spiritual renewal with 40 other priests whom I did not know. I expected the year to be a lonely one. We were all from different parts of the country. I figured we would all play it sophisticated and "cool." I didn't expect to make friends. Yet it turned out to be one of the best and deepest years of community living I had ever experienced.

It didn't begin that way. It began just as I expected: Everyone was "playing it cool," hiding behind the usual disguises, smokescreens and reserve. So was I. We effectively hid the depths of our hearts from one another—particularly the depths of our faith, our hope, our love.

Then we made a 30-day retreat. We made it in

complete silence. There were no discussions, no group-sharing sessions, no private conversations. And at the end of those 30 days we were a community. We were united in a recognized, deep, common faith, hope and love. The silence was expressive.

When I say that silence can sometimes speak louder than actions, I am talking about silence that is an action—silence that is a chosen, deep, deliberate listening to God. To see the people you live with keeping silence in this way, choosing for a time to give up conversation, reading, television, radio, the newspapers, all that could give input to their minds from the horizontal plane of this earth, and concentrating instead on listening to God—this is to see faith made visible. It is to experience community, a "common oneness" in faith.

After that there is mutual trust. There is mutual openness because of the mutual trust. And there is a sense of mutual acceptance in that which is deepest to each one: in the deep faith, hope and love which constitute the deepest, most secret reality of each one's heart and soul.

When people have found a "common unity" on the level of that which is deepest and dearest to each one, they feel a security with one another which opens the way to trusting self-revelation on other levels. Having exposed and found acceptance for their deepest selves, people are now more free to be themselves, their real selves, in front of one another. If acceptance continues, community grows.

The expression of commitment has to be credible, however. In practice, this means that the expression has to be embodied in *choices* which involve an investment of some real value.

People who give up their lives—or risk losing property, friends or freedom—in witness to the gospel are called "martyrs," that is, credible witnesses. People who give up their time or their money as an expression of love and concern for others are credible, too. Teachers who invest themselves by living out in action what they teach in the classroom are also credible. All those, and only those who express themselves through the gift, or spending, or risk or renunciation of something real and precious to them, are believable in what they say. It is on this kind of self-expression that community is founded.

Community: A Christian Need

Some of us may feel we do not need community. More than likely this is a translation of a more basic feeling that we do not want community, that we fear it, or that we see it as not worth the time or the effort.

If we feel this way, we need community! We need it because we have not yet sufficiently grasped the nature of Christianity. Over and over again Scripture describes those who have accepted the grace of Jesus Christ as being united to each other in one shared life:

Jesus describes his Church as a vine and branches (see John 15:1-8).

St. Paul uses the image of the head and members (see 1 Corinthians 12:12-31; Ephesians 1:22-23).

According to Paul, the goal and focus of Christ's mission is to draw the whole human race into the unity of one living body, which is the Body of Christ (see Ephesians 1:7-10; 4:11-13).

And when Jesus describes his Kingdom in parables, the image which predominates is that of a living organism: seed that must be nurtured to grow, a field of wheat and weeds coming to maturity, a tiny mustard seed growing into a shrub which invites the birds of the air (see Matthew 13:1-32).

It would be hard to find any justification at all in Scripture for the notion that the life of grace is something given to individuals as such and nourished within the privacy of each one's heart in isolation from all other believers. Everything, from beginning to end, is community—a common unity *experienced* in a common, shared expression of faith, hope and love:

The first thing Jesus did when he began to preach was to invite others to accompany him as he went about proclaiming the Kingdom of God (see Matthew 4:17-22). And when Jesus sent his disciples out to preach, he sent them in pairs, as a community of faith calling others into the community of faith (see Luke 10:1).

At the Last Supper Jesus prayed, more than for anything else, that his followers might be one, united in love and in faith (see John 13:34-35; 15:12; 17:20-22).

In the Acts of the Apostles we see the Church as a community:

praying together (see 1:13-14, 24; 2:1-4);

receiving the Holy Spirit together (see 2:3-4; 10:44; 19:6-7);

proclaiming the Good News of Christ together (see 2:4-14);

living and learning together (see 2:42-45);

celebrating their faith together (see 2:46-47);

healing in pairs (see 3:4, 11);

being united in mind and heart and love with each other (see 4:32-35);

supplying for each other's needs together (see 4:34-35; 11:27-30);

meeting together (see 5:12);

solving their problems together (see 6:1-6);

sending representatives in pairs to speak for them (see 8:14-17);

being instructed and baptized together (see 10:23-48);

being accountable to one another for their actions (see 11:2-4);

traveling and ministering together in pairs (see
11:22-26; 12:25; 13:2; 15:36-40);

discerning the will of God and making decisions
together (see 15:1-29);

caring for one another and expressing their emotions
together (see 20:36-38; 21:12-13; 28:15).

Without the experience of interacting deeply with
one another on the level of Christian faith, hope and love
it is almost impossible for us to relate to the early Church
as it is described in the Acts and the letters of St. Paul. It is
equally difficult for us to experience the authentic reality of
the life of grace.

The life of grace may be within us but, like
electricity, it has to flow before it is discernible. This
interaction with others in grace must take place on the
level of daily life: We express our Christian commitment
together through concrete activities, such as praying,
discussing, learning, discerning, working, singing and
celebrating together; being concerned about one another
and showing it; taking an active part in the community's
self-direction and decision-making processes; maintaining
the bond of unity through mutual accountability; taking
responsibility for clarifying whatever doubts and
questions our conduct arouses in the community; building
each other up in faith, in hope and in love.

Without this interaction we will hardly experience
what it is to love one another as Christ has loved us. We
will not experience the life of grace as a mutual giving of
new life to one another in love, or as a growing in love
through its expression "in deed and in truth" (1 John 3:18).

The choice to "form community" just means the
commitment to *give expression* to our faith, our hope, our
love as Christians *to and with* one another. It is a sharing, a
giving, of our deepest selves. It is love.

A Choice to Give Life

It is also a choice to give life. It is simply a fact that

the life of grace does not flourish as it should without the support of community. God's Word, like seed, grows best in a garden.

Even if some individual Christians could survive alone, living the life of grace in isolation without expressing it to others, the majority of Christians cannot. And survival is not health. To just "remain" a Christian is not to bear fruit as a Christian. Community is the natural milieu for the communication of Christian life.

It is also the natural milieu for that dying to self which gives life to the world. Jesus tells us,

> "…unless the grain of wheat falls to the earth and
> dies,
> it remains just a grain of wheat.
> But if it dies,
> it produces much fruit." (John 12:24)

Self-expression requires a dying to self. It necessitates a giving up of privacy, of self-enclosedness. It involves opening up to vulnerability, to possible rejection of one's deepest self, to non-appreciation of what one values most in the world.

Christ experienced this rejection. His response to it was not to close up, however; it was to open his heart even further. From the open heart of Jesus on the cross, Scripture tells us, "blood and water flowed out," the symbols of life and of pain (John 19:34).

His life and his pain, however, are the life and joy of the world:

> On the last and greatest day of the festival, Jesus
> stood up and cried out:
> "If anyone thirsts, let him come to me;
> let him drink who believes in me.
> Scripture has it:
> 'From within him rivers of living water shall
> flow.'" (John 7:37-38)

Anyone who enters into Christian community echoes that cry.

Conclusion: A Gardening Party!

This last choice—the choice to form community with others—may be the choice to begin with. Without community it is quite possible—from experience I would say it is even probable—that you will not really be able to make the choices proposed in the rest of this book. Or, if you do make them, it is unlikely you will persevere in them.

But community will get you started, and community will keep you going. If you begin by binding yourself together with someone else, or with a small group of people, in a common commitment to pray over Scripture every day, it is more than likely that you actually will begin. (This presupposes, of course, that you meet together at regular intervals to report on what you have done and share your experience of it: your successes and failures, the difficulties you encountered and the way you may have resolved them.)

If with others you face some of the specific, concrete issues that might be "thorns" in your life, values which might be in competition with the Word of God, there is more than an even chance that you will actually begin to do something about those obstacles which are blocking your spiritual growth.

Even to enter into such a community with others—to begin to interact with others in a way that is inspired by and directed toward the goals which Jesus Christ holds out to us in life—is already to make a "break" with the culture, the attitudes and values of this world. It is an act of taking a pickaxe to the "beaten path" to open it up to the seed of God's Word.

In community, and with the help of community, we will find the strength and support we need to persevere in reading Scripture and to make *choices* inspired by the words of God. Community gives us courage to take real action in response to the teaching and example of Jesus Christ.

To make such choices in response to the Word of God is to let the Kingdom come. It is to do what is required from our side to let the seed of Christ's words bear fruit in us. When, in cooperation with the Holy Spirit, we "bring Christ's words to life," in the sense of bringing them into contact with the reality of our lives, then we allow God to bring them to life in our hearts. And then we will experience the power of the Reign of God.

Summary

Theme
Christian community is a necessary support for Christian life.

Goal
To form or enter more deeply into Christian community in order to respond more fully to the Word of God.

Key Thoughts

Introduction
• What prepares us positively to receive the Word, what makes us "good soil" is "community."

What Makes a Community a Community?
• A community is just a "common unity." It exists whenever there is a common commitment which is real and is expressed in ways that are evident and credible to all.
• The essential elements of community are:

1) Two or more people
2) with a common commitment
3) who give expression to this commitment
4) in a "language" (words, symbols, actions,

choices, life-style)
5) that all the members understand
6) and that is credible.

• The key element in this definition of community is *expression*. For community to exist, the common commitment of the members must be *expressed*. And it must be expressed in language *all understand*.

Verbal and Nonverbal Expression

• Self-expression can be nonverbal. Actions speak louder than words. And sometimes silence speaks louder than actions.

• When people have found a "common unity" on the level of that which is deepest and dearest to each one, they feel a security with one another which opens the way to trusting self-revelation on other levels.

Community: A Christian Need

• Some of us may feel we do not need community. More than likely this is a translation of a more basic feeling that we do not want community—that we fear it or that we see it as not worth the time or the effort.

• Over and over again in Scripture those who have accepted the grace of Jesus Christ are described as being united to each other in one shared life.

• It would be hard to find any justification at all in Scripture for the notion that the life of grace is something given to individuals as such and nourished within the privacy of each one's heart in isolation from all other believers. Everything, from beginning to end, is community—a common unity *experienced* in a common, shared expression of faith, hope and love.

• The life of grace may be within us; but like electricity, it has to flow before it is discernible.

• This interaction with others in grace must take place on the level of daily life.

• The choice to "form community" just means the commitment to *give expression* to our faith, our hope, our love as Christians *to and with* one another. It is a sharing, a giving, of our deepest selves. It is love.

A Choice to Give Life

• Community is the natural milieu for the communication of Christian life. It is also the natural milieu for the dying to self which gives life to the world.

• Self-expression requires a dying to self. It necessitates a giving up of privacy, of self-enclosedness. It involves opening up to vulnerability, to possible rejection of one's deepest self, to non-appreciation of what one values most in the world.

Conclusion: A Gardening Party!

• Without community it is quite possible that you will not really be able to make the choices proposed in the rest of this book. Or, if you do make them, it is unlikely you will persevere in them.

• Community gives us courage to take real action in response to the teaching and example of Jesus Christ.

Questions for Reflection and Discussion

1. What experience do I have of "community"? With whom do I consciously share a "common unity" of commitment?

2. How is this common unity expressed? By the other(s)? By me?

3. Do I feel a need for community? A fear of sharing deeply with others? Does the thought of "forming community" on the spiritual level arouse a positive or a negative reaction in me? Why?

4. How can I form (or enter more deeply into) a Christian community in my home? What concrete actions would this involve?

5. What kind of community would help me most to begin and to persevere in responding to the ideas of this book? With whom could I form such a community? How would we support one another? Through what concrete actions would we give this support?

6. Do I choose to form such a community? Why? If so, what will my first step be? When will I take it?